TOM the Outback MAILMAN

Dedications

For Tom Kruse,
who carried the Australian Outback forever in his heart
KW

For my wife, Bethany
TI

TOM the Outback MAILMAN

KRISTIN WEIDENBACH • *Illustrated by* TIMOTHY IDE

LOTHIAN Children's Books

E.G.KRUSE
MARREE
LEYLAND
147-359

Big **Tom Kruse** was a **REAL AUSTRALIAN HERO**.
He delivered the mail to outback stations and towns.

He wore trousers tied up with a piece of string,
saggy leather boots without any laces,
and a shady canvas hat to shield the sun from his eyes.

He had big strong arms, sturdy legs and . . .

nine and a half fingers!

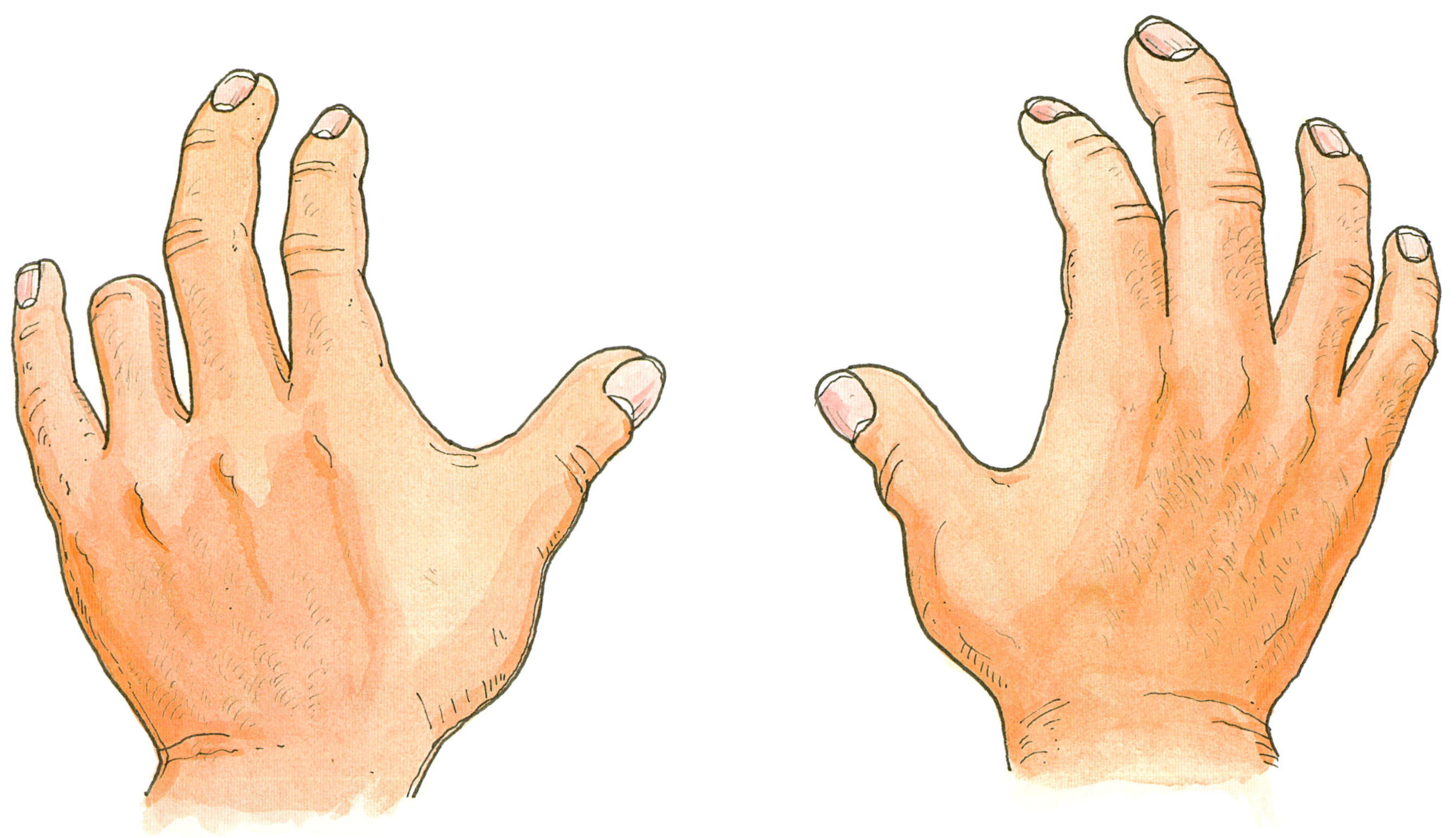

When he was little, the top of his finger got chopped off in his father's blacksmith shop. But he got used to it. "Makes one less finger to wash," said **Tom**.

Times were tough in those days, and **Tom** and his eleven brothers and sisters had to work hard . . .

harnessing horses . . .

sewing up wheat bags . . .

. . . and even smashing rocks to make new roads.

What **Tom** liked best was driving trucks.
His favourite truck was called the Badger.

He PILED IT HIGH with all manner of things . . .

bags of mail

crates of food

spare tyres

drums of petrol

furniture

a dressmaker's dummy

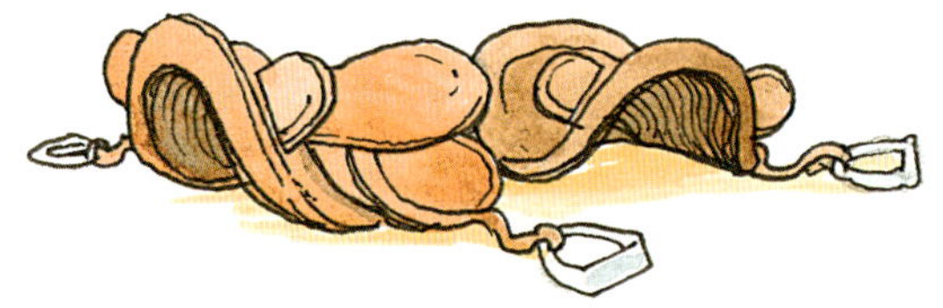

horse saddles

. . . and even some passengers **PERCHED ON TOP**.

Off they would go **UP, UP** the Birdsville Track.
It took seven days to drive from Marree . . .

. . . to Birdsville and back.

The days were **HOT**.
The sand was **DEEP**.
The flies and dust got in **Tom's** eyes.

In the stony desert, the smooth red gibbers rolled around like shiny marbles when the Badger's tyres went over them.

Tom's arms **shuddered** on the steering wheel and his teeth **CLACKED** together.

In the sandy desert, **Tom** would drive the Badger around in a **BIG** circle, going **FASTER** and **FASTER** until he could charge up the high sandhills without getting stuck.

At the top the Badger
would slither down
the other side in the
soft orange sand.

At night, **Tom** cooked his tucker on the FIRE and slept in his swag under the stars. Sometimes he camped with Jack the Dogger, who hunted for dingoes and rabbits.

One day, something unusual happened.
It started to RAIN in the outback.

The creeks and rivers began to flow. The trickles turned into a flood. Pelicans came and fish swam. Soon the water was too **DEEP** for the Badger to cross.

At OOROOWILLANIE, Mrs Scobie knitted a jumper and darned Mr Scobie's socks, while she waited for **Tom** to come.

At MUNGERANNIE, Mr Oldfield sat on his verandah, watching the rain, and waited for **Tom** to come.

At MULKA, Poddy Aiston's Buckboard ran out of petrol.

And at the end of the track,
the Birdsville Hotel ran out of beer.
Everyone waited for **Tom** to come.

Then **Tom** had a good idea.

He called the Postmaster General and asked for a boat.

In Marree, he **LOADED UP** the Badger and put the boat on top.

At the banks of the Cooper Creek,
he put the **boat in the water**.
Then, one at a time, he took all the letters and parcels,
the dummy and drums, all the boxes and barrels,
and cases and cartons, off the truck and into the boat.

Tom ferried everything to the other side of the creek.

. . . until the job was done.

On the other side of the creek, he loaded everything onto another truck, and off he went again – across the desert and over the sandhills, to the people of the Birdsville Track.

At OOROOWILLANIE, Mrs Scobie draped fabric over her new dressmaker's dummy and began to cut.

At MUNGERANNIE, Mr Oldfield **dragged** his new armchair into the lounge room and made himself comfortable with a nice cup of tea. **“AH.”**

At the MULKA Store, Poddy Aiston cranked up his car and **rattled** out of the shed.

And at Birdsville, **Tom** carried **BOXES** of beer into the Birdsville Hotel . . .

. . . and all the customers cheered.

"THREE CHEERS FOR TOM!"

"Hooray for **BIG** Tom Kruse!"

TOM'S *Outback* TRAVELS

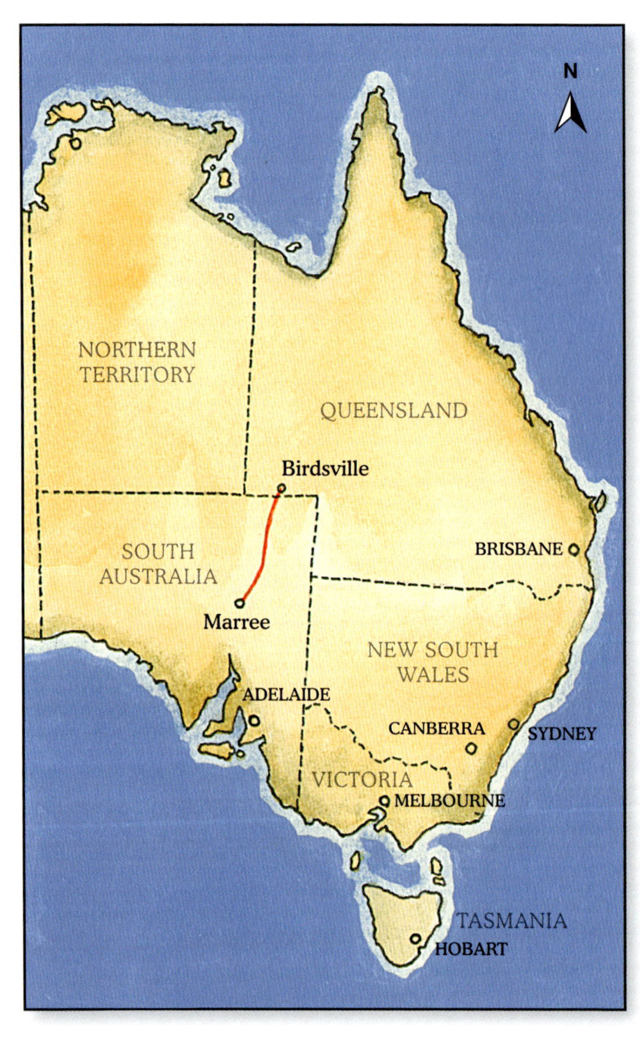

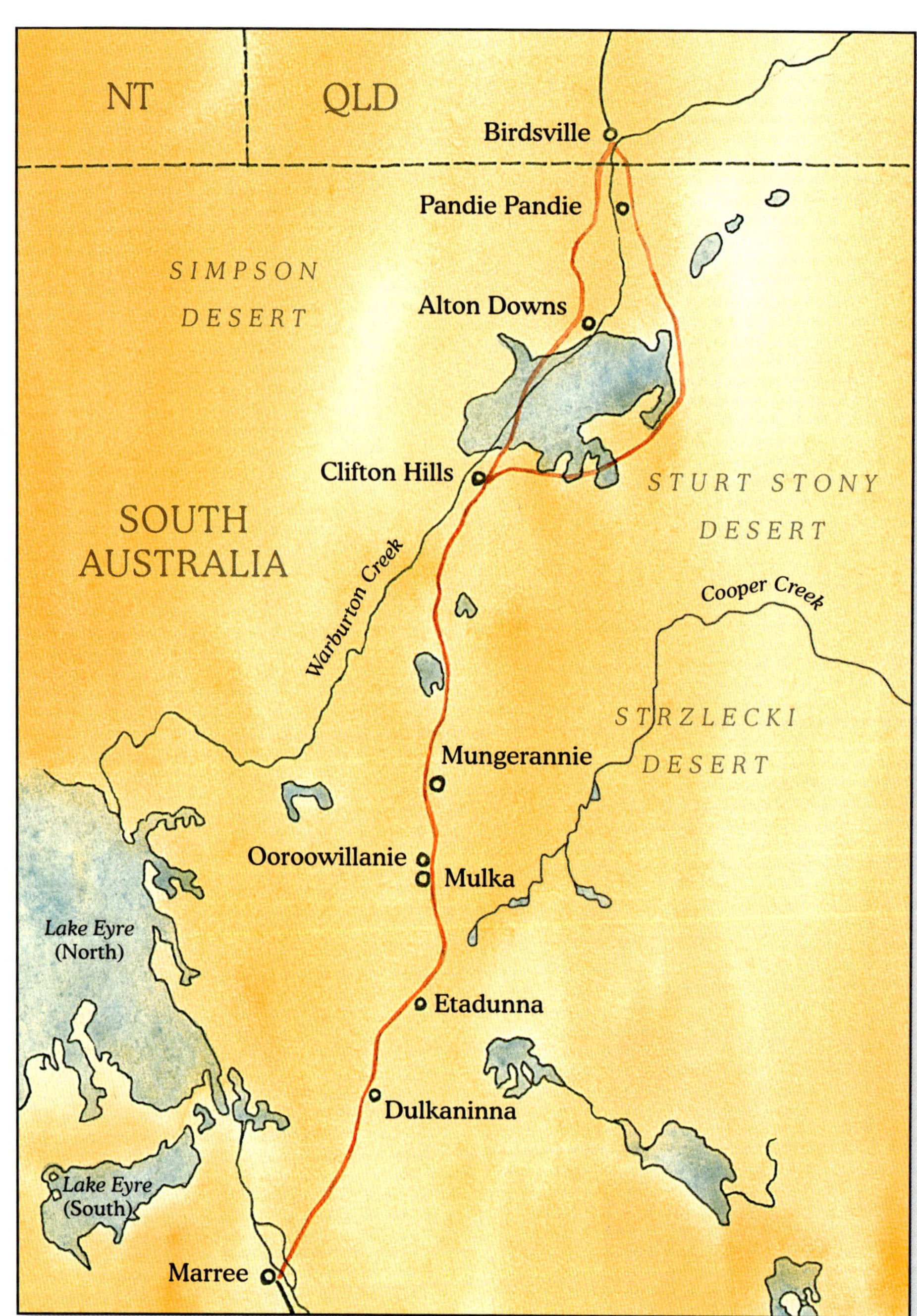

- Tom was born on 28 August 1914 at Waterloo in South Australia. He drove his first Birdsville mail run in 1936 and his last in 1963.
- You can see the real Tom Kruse delivering the mail along the Birdsville Track in a film called *The Back of Beyond*, released in 1954. The Queen saw the film and awarded Tom an MBE in recognition of his efforts to deliver the mail.
- Tom's Leyland Badger mail truck broke down near Birdsville in 1958 and became derelict. Forty years later a group of restorers helped Tom to fix it up, and in 1999 Tom drove a ceremonial last mail run. More than 2000 people sent letters to Tom to be carried on the final run.
- Tom died on 30 June 2011, aged 96. More than 750 people attended his funeral, including the Premier of South Australia, and there were tributes from all around the country to this beloved hero of the outback. Tom was pleased to know that his story would be the subject of a picture book.
- You can see Tom's Leyland Badger mail truck at the National Motor Museum at Birdwood in South Australia.
- The Birdsville Track is 500 kilometres long. It was created by big mobs of Queensland cattle walking to market in Adelaide, accompanied by drovers on horseback.
- Big tropical rains in Queensland cause the Cooper Creek to flood. When the creek was flooded Tom had to cross up to five kilometres of water that could be up to nine metres deep. All the horses and cattle had to swim across.
- The Cooper Creek floods across the Birdsville Track only once every 20 years or so. There is now a punt to ferry cars, trucks and passengers across the creek.
- The Birdsville mail is now delivered by plane. The 2,500-kilometre-round-trip route from Port Augusta in South Australia to Glengyle Station in Queensland is 'the longest mail run in the world'.

Further reading: *Mailman of the Birdsville Track: The Story of Tom Kruse* by Kristin Weidenbach (published by Hachette Australia).

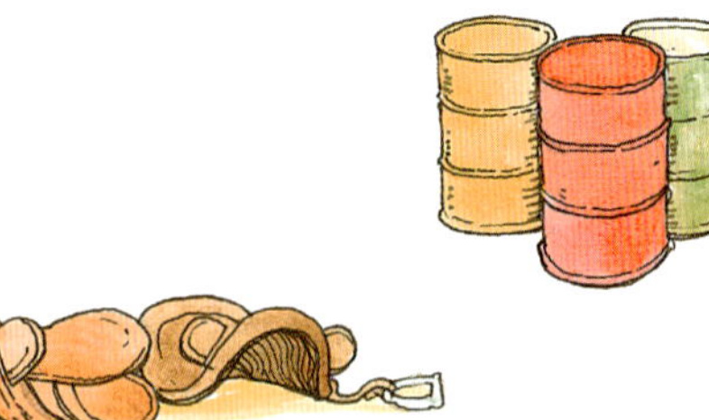

A Lothian Children's Book

First published in Australia and New Zealand in 2012
by Hachette Australia Pty Ltd
Level 17, 207 Kent Street, Sydney, NSW 2000
www.hachettechildrens.com.au

Reprinted in 2012, 2013 (four times), 2014 (twice)
This edition published in 2016

9 10 8

National Library of Australia Cataloguing-in-Publication data:

Weidenbach, Kristin, author.
Tom the outback mailman/Kristin Weidenbach; illustrated by Timothy Ide.

978 0 7336 3636 3 (paperback)

For primary school age.

Kruse, Tom.
Postal service – Birdsville Track (S. Aust. and Qld.) – Employees – Biography – Juvenile literature.
Country life – Birdsville Track (S. Aust. and Qld.) – Juvenile literature.
Birdsville Track (S. Aust. and Qld.) – Description and travel – Juvenile literature.

Ide, Timothy, illustrator.

383.49092

Designed by Kinart Pty Ltd
Colour reproduction by Splitting Image
Printed in China by Toppan Leefung